HEINEMANN
STATE STUDIES

Uniquely
Alaska

Judy A. Henry

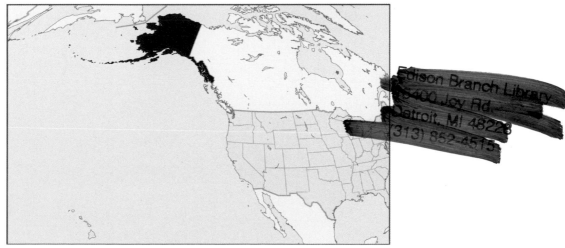

Heinemann Library
Chicago, Illinois

© 2004 Heinemann Library
a division of Reed Elsevier Inc.
Chicago, Illinois

Customer Service 888-454-2279

Visit our website at www.heinemannlibrary.com

Designed by Heinemann Library
Printed in China by WKT Company Limited.

08 07 06 05 04
10 9 8 7 6 5 4 3 2 1

**Library of Congress
Cataloging-in-Publication Data**
Henry, Judy.
  Uniquely Alaska / Judy Henry.
    v. cm. -- (Heinemann state studies)
  Includes bibliographical references and index.
  Contents: Uniquely Alaska -- Alaska's geography
and climate -- Famous firsts -- Alaska state symbols --
Alaska's history and people -- Preserving the last
frontier -- Alaska's state government -- Alaska's
culture -- Alaska's food -- Alaska's folklore and
legends.
  ISBN 1-4034-4642-3 (hc library binding) --
ISBN 1-4034-4711-X (pb)
  1. Alaska--Juvenile literature. [1. Alaska.] I. Title.
II. Series.
  F904.3.H46 2004
  979.8--dc22

                                    2003027143

Cover Pictures

Top (left to right) fishing boats, polar bears,
Alaska state flag, dogs mushing **Main**
Mendenhall Glacier

Acknowledgments
Development and photo research by
BOOK BUILDERS LLC

The author and publishers are grateful to the
following for permission to reproduce copyrighted
material:

Cover photographs by (top, L–R): Photo by James
Gritz/Alamy; Steve Bloom/Alamy; Joe Sohm/
Alamy; © Alaska Division of Tourism; (main): Ron
Niebrugge/Alamy.

Title page (L–R): Photo by Richard W. Montague/
Alaska Division of Tourism; Alaska Division of Tourism;
Alaska Division of Tourism; p. 4 Jeff Greenberg/Index
Stock Imagery; p. 5 © Division of Community &
Business Development; p. 6, 14B, 15B, 16T, 44T
Alaska Division of Tourism; p. 7 Clark James
Mischler; p. 8, 43, 45 IMA for BOOK BUILDERS
LLC; p. 10 Ron Niebrugge/Alamy; p. 11T Joe
Sohm/Alamy; p. 11B One Mile Up; p. 13T, 23T,
42B © John Hyde/Alaska Division of Tourism; p. 13B
© Mark Noble/Alaska Division of Tourism; p. 14T
© Ernst Schneider/Alaska Division of Tourism; p.
14M Christa Knijff/Alamy; p. 15T Bob Hines/
USFWS; p. 15M Eric Kamp/Index Stock Imagery;
p. 16B Mark Newman/AlaskaStock.com; p. 17T
Omni Photo Communications Inc./Index Stock
Imagery; p. 17B © Roger Angell/Alaska Division of
Tourism; p. 18 American Antiquarian Society; p. 20
Alaska and Polar Regions Department, University of
Alaska Fairbanks; p. 22 Steve Bloom/Alamy; p. 23B
Robin Hunter/USFWS; p. 25 © Mark Wayne/Alaska
Division of Tourism; p. 26 Courtesy Governor's
Office; p. 27, 30 Ken Graham/AccentAlaska.com;
p. 28 Robert Knight/eStock Photo; p. 29 Patrick J.
Endres/Alaskaphotographics.com; p. 31 Stock
Food; p. 32 B. Minton/Heinemann Library; p. 33 ©
Kristen Kimmerling/Alaska Division of Tourism; p.
34 © Richard W. Montague/Alaska Division of
Tourism; p. 35 Tracy Brooks/USFWS; p. 36 Michael
Duneen; p. 37T Courtesy UAF Athletics; p. 37B Jeff
Schultz/AlaskaStock.com; p. 39 Zefa Visual Media-
Germany/Index Stock Imagery; p. 40 James
Gritz/Alamy; p. 42T Anchorage Museum of History
& Art; p. 44B Anne Pasch.

Special thanks to Allan B. Tanner for his expert
comments in the preparation of this book.

Some words are shown in bold, **like this.**
You can find out what they mean by looking
in the glossary.

Contents

Uniquely Alaska

Alaska is unique. It is different from any other state. With more than 570,000 square miles, it is the largest of the 50 states. It is twice the size of Texas, the second-largest state and it is one-fifth the size of all the lower 48 states put together. Yet Alaska has the smallest number of people per square mile of any state—about 1.1 people per square mile. It is also the northernmost state. About one-third of Alaska lies inside the **Arctic Circle.** Alaska is the only state that is partly in the Eastern Hemisphere.

ORIGIN OF THE STATE'S NAME

The Aleut, a group of Native Americans who have lived in northwestern Alaska for thousands of years, gave the state its name. The word *Alaska* is derived from the Aleut word *Alyeska,* which means "great land."

Juneau was named for Joseph Juneau, a prospector who discovered gold in the area in 1880.

MAJOR CITIES

Juneau, the capital of Alaska, is the third-largest city in the state, with a population of 30,000. Alaska's capital city is in a remote area of the state and is one of only two U.S. capitals that can be reached only by plane or boat. Juneau is on the mainland, but mountains and the Tongass National Forest surround it. These mountains meet the sea, and avalanches, or snow slides, are dangerous threats. After the discovery of gold in the 1880s, the city quickly became the largest in the territory because the miners registered their claims and did business there. Thus, Juneau was chosen as the capital. It is the only capital located within fifteen miles of a **glacier.**

Anchorage, located in the south-central part of the state, is the largest city in Alaska, with a population of about 250,000. It is also home to about 2,000 moose and more than 200 bears. More than half of all Alaskans live nearby. Anchorage is the closest city to Denali National Park, where Mount McKinley, the highest mountain in North America, rises 20,320 feet above sea level.

Fairbanks, known as the Golden Heart of Alaska, is located in the eastern-central part of the state. The city's population is 32,000. Few people visit in winter because there is less than four hours of sunlight a day. However, in summer the sun shines up to 22 hours a day. Alaskaland Pioneer Theme Park, located in Fairbanks, with its log cabins, gold rush towns, early Alaskan Native and Indian dwellings, and a **frontier** stampede allow visitors to experience Alaska's past. The University of Alaska at Fairbanks Museum includes artifacts from mining operations and **fossils** from the area.

Fairbanks, once a city of tents, grew rapidly after Felix Pedro discovered gold in the area in 1902.

Alaska's Geography and Climate

Alaska is located in the northwestern corner of North America. It is bordered on the west by the Pacific Ocean, on the north by the Arctic Ocean, and to the east and south by Canada.

Alaska is 1,480 miles long and 810 miles wide. It includes hundreds of islands, arctic **tundra,** 5,000 glaciers, and four mountain ranges. The state is home to more than 3 million lakes and 3,000 streams. In addition, Alaska has more than 33,600 miles of seacoast, which is 50 percent more than the rest of the U.S. coastlines combined.

Although wildflowers grow in summer, the tundra is barren most of the year.

LAND

Alaska has four land regions. These are the Pacific Mountain System, the Central Uplands and Lowlands, the Rocky Mountain System of Alaska, and the Arctic Coastal Plain.

The Pacific Mountain System is found in the south and southeast parts of Alaska and includes the Aleutian Islands, which stretch 400 miles along the Pacific Coast. This region borders the Gulf of Alaska and the Pacific Ocean. Glacier Bay National Park and the Mendenhall and Malaspina glaciers, among the state's largest, are located there. Denali National Park's Mount McKinley is located

Giant Vegetables

Since 1941, when a giant cabbage weighed in at 23 pounds, farmers in the Matanuska Valley have worked to grow gigantic vegetables with the hope of winning a $2,000 cash prize. The largest cabbage ever weighed 124 pounds. Because the earth's tilt is toward the sun during the summer, long sunlit days warm Alaska between May 10 and August 2 and the sun shines for about 20 hours a day. Some farmers give their crops extra special care. In Palmer, Alaska, during the summer of 2003, farmer Scott Robb used air conditioning in plastic pipes with holes to protect his crops from heat, plastic sheeting to protect them from the wind, and electric fencing to keep out moose.

in this region. Lowland areas include the Matanuska Valley, a rich farmland.

The Central Uplands and Lowlands is the largest region in Alaska. To the south is the Alaska Mountain Range. The Brooks Mountain Range is in the north. On its western border is Canada. Seward **Peninsula** in southwest Alaska is in this region. This area has rolling hills and swampy river valleys. Among the major rivers is the Yukon River, which, at 1,875 miles, is the third-longest river in the United States.

The Rocky Mountain System of Alaska is north of the Central Uplands and Lowlands. It includes the Brooks Mountain Range and its foothills. It has mountains made by glaciers that are 9,000 feet above sea level. Farthest north in Alaska is the Arctic Coastal Plain. The land there is known as **permafrost** and remains frozen for much of the year. However, the ground's surface thaws in the spring. This thawed ground is called tundra. In the far northwest, the Bering **Strait** separates Alaska from the continent of Asia and connects the northern Pacific Ocean with the Arctic Ocean.

CLIMATE

Alaska's climate is varied. Southeastern Alaska is mild and wet, with up to 200 inches of **precipitation** each year. Northern Alaska is colder and receives less than seven inches of precipitation. The coastlines are considered **temperate.** In the Arctic Coastal areas, high winds are common and can cause **whiteouts.** Central Alaska is dry and receives very little rain. The highest recorded temperature in the state is 100°F. It was recorded on June 27, 1915, at Fort Yukon. The lowest recorded temperature is –80°F. This temperature was recorded at Prospect Creek Camp on January 23, 1971.

Precipation in Alaska can vary greatly even within a city. Downtown Juneau receives nearly twice as much precipitation each year (93 inches) as Juneau airport (53 inches).

Average Annual Precipitation Alaska

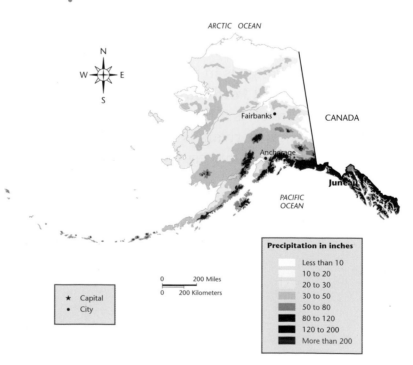

ARCTIC OCEAN

N
W E
S

Fairbanks•

CANADA

Anchorage
•

Juneau★

PACIFIC OCEAN

0   200 Miles
0   200 Kilometers

★ Capital
• City

Precipitation in inches

Less than 10
10 to 20
20 to 30
30 to 50
50 to 80
80 to 120
120 to 200
More than 200

Famous Firsts

HISTORIC FIRSTS

In 1842, Russian scientists in Sitka, the Russian capital of Alaska, founded the Sitka Magnetic **Observatory,** the first on the west coast. From the observatory, scientists studied **meteors** and **magnetic phenomenon,** such as the Northern Lights. In 1904, the observatory began studying earthquakes. Each year Alaska has about 5,000 earthquakes, with 1,000 rating higher than a 3.5 on the **Richter scale.** Of the ten strongest earthquakes in the world since 1900, three were in Alaska. The observatory remains one of the world's most important observation stations.

MILITARY FIRSTS

Attu Island in the Aleutians is the site of the only **World War II** (1939–1945) battles fought on the North American continent. Its location was important during the war because Attu is 1,100 miles west of Alaska's mainland but only 750 miles northeast of Japan's Kurile Islands.

Battle for the Aleutian Islands

Attu and Kiska were occupied by the Japanese in June 1942. The United States, with 11,000 troops, attacked 2,400 Japanese troops to regain control in May 1943. The battle lasted eighteen days and resulted in 549 U.S. deaths and 1,148 injuries. Today, battlements, storage vaults, and a now-sealed underground hospital remind visitors of this attack. Fort Abercrombie State Park, a military establishment, was the setting for the first secret radar installation in World War II.

GEOGRAPHICAL FIRSTS

The Mendenhall Glacier began retreating in the mid-1700s, but it will take hundreds more years for it to disappear.

Alaska's **glaciers** make up 75,000 square miles of glacial ice. Several ice fields have glaciers more than 4,500 feet thick. The Mendenhall Glacier is a type of glacier known as a piedmont glacier, which is a large valley glacier of slowly moving ice. The Mendenhall Glacier is twelve miles long and three miles wide. It is one of the largest piedmont glaciers, with a front edge height of 200 feet. Another glacier type is a tidewater glacier, which is a mountain glacier that ends at the ocean. The Bering Glacier is the longest in Alaska, at more than 122 miles long. Glacier Bay has more tidewater glaciers than anywhere else on Earth.

Alaska is home to Mount McKinley, the tallest mountain in North America. It is 20,320 feet above sea level. It is so tall that on many days the top is not visible because of the clouds in the high elevations. The state is also home to seventeen of the twenty highest U.S. mountains.

One in ten earthquakes worldwide occur in Alaska. The Great American Alaskan earthquake occurred in south-central Alaska on March 27, 1964, and lasted four minutes. Its Richter scale reading of 9.3 makes it the largest earthquake to hit the United States in recorded history and one of the largest worldwide. It killed 115 people and left 4,500 people homeless.

Alaska's State Symbols

ALASKA STATE FLAG

In 1926, thirteen-year-old Benny Benson of Cognac designed the state flag. The territorial government adopted it on May 2, 1927, and it became the official state flag in 1959. Its gold stars stand for the constellation known as the Big Dipper, or Ursa Major.

The blue color symbolizes sky, water, and wildflowers.

ALASKA STATE SEAL

Although the District of Alaska adopted a seal in 1884, the governor redesigned the seal in 1910 to highlight Alaska's resources and industries. The smelter represents mining, the trees represent timberland, the farmer represents agriculture, and the seals and fish represent commercial fishing. When Alaska entered the Union in 1959, the word *territory* on the seal was changed to *state*.

The rays above the mountains stand for the Northern Lights.

STATE MOTTO: "NORTH TO THE FUTURE"

The Alaskan state motto is "North to the Future." This means that Alaska is a land of promise. Richard Peter, a Juneau journalist, created the motto. He felt that it should remind Alaskans to look to the future because the state has much to give to its people. The Alaska state motto was adopted in 1967.

STATE NICKNAME: THE LAST FRONTIER

Alaska's official nickname is the Last Frontier because of its opportunities for Alaska's people. Alaska is sparsely populated, so its vast wilderness areas make it seem like an unsettled frontier.

STATE SONG: "ALASKA'S FLAG"

Alaska's territorial government adopted "Alaska's Flag" as the state song in 1955. Marie Drake, an educational employee, wrote the first verse. Elinor Dusenbury wrote the music. In 1986, Carol Beery Davis wrote the second verse because the native Alaskans were concerned that they had not been mentioned in the first verse. The University of Alaska holds the copyright.

"Alaska's Flag"

Eight stars of gold on a field of blue—
Alaska's flag. May it mean to you
The blue of the sea, the evening sky,
The mountain lakes, and the flow'rs nearby;
The gold of the early sourdough dreams,
The precious gold of the hills and streams;
The brilliant stars in the northern sky,
The *Bear*—the *Dipper*—and, shining high,
the great North Star with its steady light,
Over land and sea a beacon bright.
Alaska's flag—to Alaskans dear,
The simple flag of a last frontier.

A Native lad chose the Dipper's stars
For Alaska's flag that there be no bars
Among our cultures. Let it be known
Through years the Native's past has grown
To share life's treasures, hand in hand,
to keep Alaska our Great-Land;
We love the northern midnight sky,
the mountains, lakes and streams nearby.
The great North Star with its steady light
will guide all cultures, clear and bright,
with nature's flag to Alaskan's dear,
the simple flag of the last frontier.

STATE TREE: SITKA SPRUCE

In 1962 Alaska selected the Sitka spruce as the state tree. The Sitka spruce is named after the Russian capital of Alaska. It can grow to about 230 feet in height and more than 6 ½ feet in width.

STATE BIRD: WILLOW PTARMIGAN

In 1955 Alaska adopted the willow ptarmigan as the state bird. In summer the willow ptarmigan has brown feathers, but in winter, it is covered with white feathers. These colors help the bird to blend into its surroundings and so protect it from predators.

STATE FISH: KING SALMON

In 1962 Alaska selected the king salmon as the state fish. These salmon range from 50 to 120 pounds. King salmon live in the northern Pacific Ocean, but travel up to 1,500 miles upstream to lay their eggs.

The Sitka spruce is the largest spruce tree and keeps its color all year long.

When adult king salmon lay their eggs in fresh water, they are prey to bears, who frequently eat the large fish.

Forget-Me-Nots grow from five to twelve inches high.

The four spot skimmer dragonfly is a unique flier with helicopter-like wings.

Moose antlers, which are found only on males, can reach a spread of five feet or more.

STATE FLOWER: FORGET-ME-NOT

In 1917 the territorial government selected the forget-me-not as Alaska's state flower. It has a yellow center with blue petals and grows wild in many areas of the state. The forget-me-not blooms from late June to late July.

STATE INSECT: FOUR SPOT SKIMMER DRAGONFLY

In 1995 Alaskan schoolchildren selected the four spot skimmer dragonfly as the state insect. With its ability to hover and fly forward and backward, it reminds the Alaskan people of a helicopter.

STATE LAND MAMMAL: MOOSE

In 1998 Alaska selected the moose as the state land mammal. At six feet tall, the moose is the largest member of the deer family, and it is the most hunted animal in the state.

Bowhead whales almost disappeared because of commercial fishing, but now they are protected by the government.

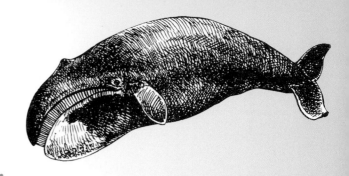

STATE SEA MAMMAL: BOWHEAD WHALE

Alaska selected the bowhead whale as the state sea mammal in 1983. These whales stay in the freezing waters of the Arctic all year. In 2004, there were more than 10,000 bowhead whales. Their numbers continue to increase every year.

STATE MINERAL: GOLD

In 1968 Alaska selected gold as the state mineral. Gold was first discovered in Alaska in 1880 near Juneau. The search for gold played an important part in Alaska's history.

Today Alaska mines more gold than any other state in the nation.

STATE SPORT: DOG MUSHING

In 1972 Alaska's lawmakers selected dog mushing, or sledding, as the state sport. The sport recalls the times

Dog mushing continues today with races held throughout the state.

Many people believe that jade brings good health.

when dog sleds provided transportation across the frozen **tundra** and snow-covered flatlands and mountains.

STATE GEM: JADE

In 1968 Alaska selected jade as its state gem. Most Alaskan jade is found in the Jade Mountains in the northwestern part of the state. It comes in a variety of colors, including green, brown, black, yellow, white, and red. A large deposit of dark green jade is located on the Seward Peninsula. Only one-fourth of mined jade is jewelry quality. The rest is used in clock faces, bookends, and tabletops.

Woolly mammoths were members of the elephant family.

STATE FOSSIL: WOOLY MAMMOTH

In 1986 Alaska selected the woolly mammoth as the state **fossil.** Woolly mammoths roamed the northern plains for 2 million years, until about 10,000 years ago. Woolly mammoth fossils have been found in Alaska's thawing permafrost.

Alaska's History and People

NATIVE PEOPLE

The first people may have arrived in western Alaska about 15,000 years ago. They hunted bowhead whales, seals, fish, and caribou for food and bones. They used wood products for tools, boats, and cooking items.

EARLY EXPLORERS

In 1725 Russia's ruler, Peter the Great, sent Vitus Bering from Denmark to explore the North Pacific. In 1728 Bering entered the waters now known as the Bering Strait. Bering, along with scientist George Wilhelm Steller, explored the area. Later, in 1741, Bering and Alexey Chirikov explored mainland Alaska and the Aleutian Islands. These voyages established Russia's claims to Alaska.

Fishing remains an important part of Native Alaskan culture.

The first Russian Orthodox mission was established in Alaska in 1794. The people worshipped and followed their beliefs at this mission and Orthodox

The Holy Transfiguration of Our Lord Church in Ninilchik was one of the first churches in Alaska.

priests worked to convert the Native Alaskans to Christianity. Later, as the number of Russian settlers grew, more Russian Orthodox missions and churches were built.

In 1742 Russian explorers and settlers came to Alaska to explore the area and hunt animals for fur. Alexander Baranov managed the Russian American Company and served as Russia's governor of Alaska from 1799 to 1819.

Alaska and the Civil War

The **Confederate** ship, the CSS *Shenandoah*, fired the last shot of the U.S. Civil War (1861–1865) near St. Lawrence Island on June 22, 1865. This was nearly two months after the rest of the South had surrendered. The crew had journeyed to Alaska to attack Yankee whaling ships.

THE PURCHASE OF ALASKA

By 1859, however, Russia's ruler, Alexander II, had become disappointed with the Alaskan lands. Alaska was a long way from the Russian capital, St. Petersburg, and maintaining the colony was costing too much. In addition, few riches were found. He then began talks with the United States to purchase Alaska. Because of the **Civil War** (1861–1865) in the United States, no agreement was reached until 1867.

Before Alaska became a state, some cartoons joked about bears ("Ursus" in Latin) casting votes in political elections.

On March 30, 1867, U.S. Secretary of State William Seward signed an agreement for the United States to purchase Alaska for $7,200,000. The cost was only about 2 cents per acre. Seward pushed the United States to buy Alaska, despite its distance from the rest of the country. Many Americans opposed the purchase because they thought Alaska was a frozen wasteland, home to polar bears and seals. Some who believed the United States made a mistake called Alaska "Seward's Folly" and "Seward's Ice Box."

THE ALASKA TERRITORY, 1912

Soon after Alaska became a part of the United States, explorers began to move north in search of riches and adventure. An Alaskan explorer, William H. Dall, created the first map of the entire Yukon River. Later, Lieutenant Fredcrick Schwatka and Henry T. Allen explored other parts of the area. In 1880, many Americans quickly developed an interest in Alaska when Joe Juneau discovered gold near what is today the city of Juneau. Juneau's discovery soon became the largest gold mine in the world. In 1898, 30,000 miners and adventurers arrived in southeastern Alaska and set up small mining towns hoping to strike it rich. Tent cities sprung up overnight but were abandoned if gold was not found. Many miners moved on, hoping to strike it rich at another site. Some people stayed and set up lumber and fishing businesses. In 1912, Congress made Alaska a territory with an elected legislature.

STATEHOOD

In 1916, the first of many **bills** calling for Alaskan statehood was introduced into Congress, and all these early bills failed. In 1949, an Alaskan Statehood Committee was formed. This group worked with government leaders, newspaper editors, and others to convince Congress to make Alaska a state. In 1950, a statehood bill passed the U.S. House of Representatives but failed in the Senate. Finally, Alaska became the 49th state in the

The 49-star flag

After Alaska's admission to the Union, a 49th star was added to the American flag. This flag had seven rows of seven stars. However, it remained in use for only about eight months—until August 1959, when Hawaii became the 50th state.

Union on January 3, 1959. It was the first state outside the **contiguous** United States.

FAMOUS PEOPLE

B. Frank Heintzleman (1888–1965), governor. In 1918, Frank Heintzleman worked in the Tongass National Forest as the regional forester for the Alaska Region of the Forest Service. He helped to establish the first pulp mills at Ketchikan and Sitka, which helped the area's economy grow. He later served as territorial governor (1953–1957).

Carl Ben Eielson (1897–1929), pilot. Carl Eielson, born in North Dakota, was the first pilot in Alaska, and he worked for the Farthest North Aviation Company. At first, he delivered the U.S. Mail and then he made commercial flights. He later became an Alaskan **bush pilot.** Although an experienced pilot, he got lost and died in a blizzard. A mountain peak near Mount McKinley is named after him.

Margaret Elizabeth Bell (1898–1990), author. Margaret Bell was born in Thorn Bay. As an adult, she moved to an abandoned town near Ketchikan. Among her best-known books is *Ride Out the Storm* (1951), which is based on her childhood.

William A. Egan (1914–1984), governor. William Egan served as Alaska's first elected state governor from 1959 to 1966, and again from 1970 to 1974. He was born in Valdez and served as the mayor of that

In 1971 William A. Egan (on right) was named Alaskan of the Year.

city from 1943 to 1946. He also served in the Territorial Congress as both a representative and a senator.

Joe Redington, Sr. (1917–1999), dogsled musher and promoter. Joe Redington, Sr. arrived in Alaska in 1948 from Pennsylvania. He raised and raced sled dogs and helped to promote the **Iditarod** Trail Sled Dog Race. In 1997, he celebrated the 25th anniversary of this race at the age of 80. He died two years later and was buried in Wasilla, Alaska, in his favorite dogsled.

Walter J. Hickel (1919–   ), governor. Walter Hickel was born in Kansas but led the fight for Alaskan statehood. He served as governor twice, from 1966 to 1968 and again from 1990 to 1994. In 1969 and 1970, Hickel served as Secretary of the Interior under President Richard Nixon. He was a strong environmentalist, and he supported safety in petroleum drilling and pipeline construction. He is the author of *Who Owns America?* (1971).

Tommy Moe (1970–   ), skier. From Palmer, Tommy Moe was the first U.S. skier to win two medals during a single Olympics. In the 1994 Winter Olympics in Lillehammer, Norway, he won a gold medal in the men's downhill and a silver medal in the super G. He is now retired.

Jewel (1974–   ), singer. Jewel, whose full name is Jewel Kilcher, was born in Utah, but her family moved to Alaska shortly after her birth. By 1995, she had written and recorded her first top-selling CD, *Pieces of You*. She continues to sing and perform around the world.

Preserving the Last Frontier

Alaska's nickname is the "Last Frontier." Much of the state is a vast unspoiled wilderness, where animals run free and plants grow wild—as they have done for thousands of years.

Polar bears are found in the Arctic region of Alaska.

THE NATIONAL WILDLIFE REFUGE

Tucked away in Alaska's northeast corner, the National Wildlife Refuge is a 19.6 million-acre wildlife sanctuary where the government protects animals and plants. It is a sweeping expanse of **tundra** interrupted by rivers. The refuge is located between the foothills of the Brooks Range and the waters of the Beaufort Sea. About 160 types of birds, mammals, such as grizzly bears, wolverines, wolves, and arctic foxes, and marine animals including whales and other species thrive in the region. To preserve the environment, most areas of the Arctic National Wildlife Refuge are closed to gas and oil exploration.

Oil Spill!

On March 24, 1989, an Exxon oil company's ship, the *Valdez,* ran aground on Alaska's southern coast. The accident caused 11 million gallons, or 257,000 barrels, of oil to leak into Prince William Sound. The oil damaged 1,300 miles of shoreline and killed about 250,000 seabirds, 2,800 sea otters, 300 harbor seals, 250 bald eagles, 22 killer whales, and billions of salmon and herring eggs.

PRESERVING ALASKA'S RAIN FOREST

Alaska's rain forest covers a 1,000-mile stretch of coastline from Ketchikan to Kodiak. With more than 5 million acres of old-growth forest, it is one of the world's largest remaining **temperate** rain

Alaska's rain forest, located in southeastern Alaska, provides a shelter for bears.

forests. The region is home to many rare animals, including brown bears, bald eagles, wolves, and all five species of Pacific salmon. Because more people are moving to the area and want to use the rain forest's resources, it is in danger. An international organization, the World Resources Institute, has recognized Alaska's rain forest as one of the world's last threatened frontier forests.

SAVING ENDANGERED SPECIES

Alaska is unique among the states because it has been able to keep nearly all of its native animals and plants thriving. Because of the state's geographical location, limited development, small farming industry, and conservation laws, native plants and animals have prospered. Many species, such as the grizzly bear and the gray wolf, flourish in Alaska. For example, of the 50,000 bald eagles in the United States, about 80 percent soar over Alaska. With continued careful management and adequate habitat protection, these species will be preserved for years to come.

*In May 1993, the Alaska Department of Fish and Game listed the blue whale and humpback whale as **endangered** species.*

Alaska's State Government

Alaska's government is based in Juneau, the capital. Similar to the **federal government** in Washington, D.C., Alaska's government is made up of three branches—the legislative, the executive, and the judicial branch.

The state's constitution, or plan of government, was written in 1956, three years before Alaska became a state. It promises many freedoms for Alaska's people—including freedom of religion, speech, and the press. These basic rights are based on those listed in the U.S. Constitution.

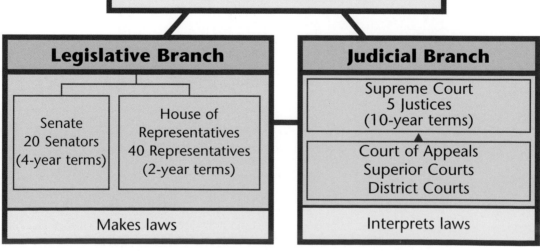

Executive Branch

Governor
(4-year term)

Lieutenant Governor
(4-year term)

Attorney General
(4-year term)

Carries out the laws of the state

Legislative Branch

Senate
20 Senators
(4-year terms)

House of
Representatives
40 Representatives
(2-year terms)

Makes laws

Judicial Branch

Supreme Court
5 Justices
(10-year terms)

Court of Appeals
Superior Courts
District Courts

Interprets laws

THE LEGISLATIVE BRANCH

The legislative branch makes the laws for Alaska. It is divided into the house of representatives and the senate. The 40 representatives in the house serve 2-year terms and must be at least 21 years old. The 20 senators serve for 4 years and must be at least 25 years old. Both must be **residents** of the state for at least three years and live in the district from which they were elected for at least one year. Alaska's lawmakers hold two regular sessions each year, usually during January through May.

A **bill,** or proposed law, may start in either house of the legislature. A bill must be approved by a **majority,** or more than half, of the members of both houses before it can be sent to the governor for approval. If the governor signs the bill, it becomes a law. If the governor **vetoes,** or rejects, the bill, it does not become a law. The legislature may override the governor's veto of most bills by a two-thirds majority vote. Bills relating to money and taxes must be overridden by a three-fourths majority vote.

The second floor of the state capitol displays a photographic history of Alaska from 1893 to 1945.

THE EXECUTIVE BRANCH

The executive branch enforces the laws and runs the state from day to day. The governor is the head of this branch. The governor is limited to two four-year terms in a row. However, voters may reelect the governor again, after time out of the office. The lieutenant governor is second in command, and takes over if the governor is not able to complete his or her term. The lieutenant governor, whose term of office is the same as the governor, helps the governor run the state. The Alaskan people also elect an attorney general to a four-year term

Governor Frank H. Murkowski, formerly a U.S. Senator for 22 years, regularly visits with Alaska's students.

of office. The governor appoints department heads, who must then be approved by both houses in the legislature.

THE JUDICIAL BRANCH

The main purpose of the judicial branch is to make sure the state's constitution is being followed. Alaska's court system has four levels of state courts—the district courts, the superior courts, the **appeals** court, and the supreme court. District courts and superior courts are trial courts. The appeals court and the supreme court review decisions made in the two lower courts.

The district courts have seventeen judges who hear misdemeanor cases. These are cases involving crimes that are less serious than **felony** crimes. The governor appoints the district court judges. However, each district court judge must run in a **retention** election at the first general election held more than two years after he or she was appointed. District judges must then run for election every four years.

The superior court has thirty-four judges who hear civil cases and criminal cases with a felony charge. After being appointed by the governor, each superior court judge must run for election. Voters in the judge's judicial district make their choice in the first election held more than three years after the judge's appointment. Thereafter, each judge must run again every six years.

Three judges make up the court of appeals. The chief judge is appointed by the chief justice of the supreme court to a two-year term. Each court of appeals judge is subject to approval or rejection by a majority of voters statewide on a **nonpartisan ballot** at the first general election held more than three years after his or her appointment. Thereafter, each judge must run in an election every eight years.

The court of appeals meets in Anchorage, but often travels to Fairbanks. It can hear appeals in cases involving criminal prosecutions, juvenile delinquency, probation, parole, and bail.

The supreme court, the highest court in the state, sets the administrative rules for all courts. It makes final decisions in civil and criminal cases based on Alaska's constitution. The governor appoints the justices to the court. Each supreme court justice is subject to approval or rejection by a majority of voters on a nonpartisan ballot at the first general election held more than three years after appointment. Thereafter, each justice must run in a retention election every ten years. The five justices select one of their members by majority vote to be the chief justice. The chief justice holds that office for three years and may not serve consecutive terms.

The state supreme court justices hear cases in Anchorage (shown here) every month and in Fairbanks and Juneau every three months.

Alaska's Culture

The people of Alaska preserve and educate others with their native arts and festivals. Alaskan natives pass on their culture by continuing the activities of their people.

The totem pole tells stories of a clan's history by using animal carvings.

ALASKA'S NATIVE ARTS

Native Alaskans create their art for practical and cultural uses. One art form, the **totem** pole, is carved out of cedar wood and can be as tall as 60 feet.

Blankets may take up to a year to make and be used for warmth, which is their practical purpose. They also are used in dances to tell stories of activities such as whale hunting. In the blanket toss, people hold onto the blanket, and a small child is tossed into the air to look ahead for animals to be hunted. Today, the blanket toss continues as a fun activity at local festivals. Native Alaskans make other native art, such as fans, masks, ivory **scrimshaws,** whale bone carvings, and woodcarvings. Difficult woven baskets may take up to fifteen hours to make.

The Fairbanks Festival of Native Arts features ceremonies and feasts to celebrate the winter solstice, which is the shortest day of the year in the northern hemisphere.

Every February, the city of Fairbanks hosts the Festival of Native Arts. The festival was started in 1973 by the students at the University of Alaska at Fairbanks in order to bring together the state's native cultural groups. The festival showcases the many aspects of native Alaskan culture that make the state unique. Artists and craftspeople share their talents with one another and the many people who attend the event.

Established in 1799, Sitka is the oldest city in Alaska. Located in southeastern Alaska, it was once the capital of the Russian colony. Visitors to Sitka can still see the onion-domed tops and golden crosses that are part of Russian Orthodox churches. There are 26 Orthodox churches and 59 Orthodox chapels throughout this part of Alaska. One of the most famous churches in the area is St. Michael's Cathedral.

Carvers create ice sculptures at the Fur Rondy.

THE FUR RONDY

In Anchorage each February, a ten-day festival celebrates the time when trappers met to buy and sell furs. It opens with the Miners' and Trappers' Ball, which is a large costume party. The festival holds an auction for bear, beaver, wolf, and moose furs, and features the World Championship Sled Dog Race. In the Rondy Weight Pull, sled dogs pull weighted sleds for several yards—and the weights may reach 1,000 pounds. Another unique activity at the festival is the softball tournament in **snowshoes.**

UNIQUE HOLIDAYS

Seward's Day is celebrated on the last Monday in March. It celebrates the treaty signing that marked the U.S. purchase of the Alaska Territory from Russia. It is named for Secretary of State William Seward, who led the actions to purchase Alaska.

Each year on October 18, Alaska Day is held. This date is the anniversary of the formal transfer of the Alaskan Territory from Russia to the United States. Alaska Day celebrates the taking down of the Russian flag and the raising of the U.S. flag at Sitka, the original Russian capital city.

Alaska's Food

Alaskan foods include numerous freshwater and salt-water fish, such as salmon, halibut, and king crab. Alaskans also eat foods that are hunted, such as moose and caribou, as well as fruits and vegetables.

BOUNTY FROM THE SEA

Alaska's cold oceans and seas are filled with a wide variety of fish and seafood. Salmon, herring, trout, northern pike, rockfish, and crab are among the most popular catches.

BAKED ALASKA

The dessert known as Baked Alaska was not invented in Alaska, but one story tells of a famous New York chef creating the sweet treat in honor of Seward's 1867 purchase. A news article of the time described the newly invented Baked Alaska. The article described the frozen dessert as a tall, cone-shaped mold of banana and vanilla ice cream. It was placed on a hollowed-out cake base that was filled with apricot marmalade. Before the dessert was served, the chef covered it with meringue and browned it in a hot oven.

Baked Alaska is popular throughout the world.

Sockeye Salmon Chowder

It is believed that salmon was originally called *sau-kie,* meaning "chief of fishes," by the Native Alaskans. Many people feel that Sockeye salmon is the best tasting of all salmon. **Ask an adult to help you with this recipe.**

4 slices bacon, diced

1 carrot, diced fine

1 onion, diced fine

1 stalk celery, diced fine

1 15 ounce can of clams, chopped and undrained

4 potatoes, diced

1 cup water

2 1/2 tablespoons fresh dill

2 tablespoons chopped garlic

1 tablespoon chopped fresh basil

1 1/2 teaspoons thyme

1/2 teaspoon oregano

4 cups heavy cream

3/4 pound sockeye salmon fillet, coarsely chopped (can be raw, cooked fresh, or leftover) or canned salmon

4 cups milk

1/2 cup cornstarch

salt and pepper

In a four-quart stockpot, sauté bacon until it starts to get clear. Add carrot, onion, and celery. Sauté until onion is clear. Add clams with their juice, potatoes, and water. Cook at a slow boil until potatoes are tender. Add dill, garlic, basil, thyme, oregano, heavy cream, and salmon. Cook for 15 minutes, stirring constantly. Mix milk with cornstarch. Add mixture to the soup, stirring constantly. Cook until soup thickens. Salt and pepper to taste. Serve immediately. Serves eight to ten.

Alaska's Folklore and Legends

Alaskans have passed down folklore and legends from one generation to the next. Some of the stories are tall tales, and others are true stories.

THE FIRST TEARS

The Inuit people tell of a man who set out one day to hunt seal so he could provide food for his wife and son who remained in camp. As the man approached the shore, he was happy to see many seals. They would supply his family with plenty of food. However, as he came nearer, the seals quietly slipped into the water. Only one large seal remained on the shore.

Before stories were written down, oral storytelling allowed history to be passed on to new generations.

As the man crept softly toward the lone seal, it too slipped into the water. The man experienced a strange emotion. He felt water in his eyes. He touched his eyes and tasted salty water, just like the water in the sea. He also had unknown sounds coming from his mouth and chest.

His wife and son heard him and came running to see what was wrong. They too saw the water in the man's eyes. As the man told of his hunt for the seals and that every seal had escaped, the wife and son also had water

in their eyes. This is known to the Inuit people as the first time a person cried. Following this, the man and son always hunted seal together.

THE HOUSEDOG AND THE WOLF

The moon was shining very bright one night when a half-starved wolf, whose ribs were almost sticking through his skin, chanced to meet a plump, well-fed housedog. After greeting each other, the wolf inquired, "How is it, cousin dog, that you look so contented? Try as I may, I can barely find enough food to keep me from starvation."

"Alas, cousin wolf," said the housedog, "you lead too irregular a life. Why do you not work as steadily as I do?"

"I would gladly work steadily if I could get a place," said the wolf.

"That's easy," replied the dog. "Come with me to my master's house and help me keep the thieves away at night."

"Gladly," said the wolf, "for as I am living in the woods I am having a sorry time of it. There is nothing like a roof over one's head and a belly full of food at hand."

"Follow me," said the dog.

While they were trotting along together, the wolf spied a mark on the dog's neck. Out of curiosity, he asked what had caused it.

"Oh, that's nothing much," replied the dog. "Perhaps my collar was a little tight, the collar to which my chain is fastened—"

"Chain!" cried the wolf in surprise. "You don't mean to tell me that you are not free to rove where you please?"

"Why, not exactly," said the dog, somewhat shame-facedly. "You see, my master thinks I am a bit fierce, and ties me up in the daytime. But he lets me run free at night. I get plenty of sleep during the day so that I can watch better at night. I really am a great favorite at the house. The master feeds me off his own plate, and the servants are continually offering me handouts from the kitchen. But wait, where are you going?"

As the wolf started back toward the forest, he said, "Good night to you, my poor friend. You are welcome to your food—and your chains. As for me, I prefer my freedom to your fat."

Alaska's Sports Teams

Alaska's largest college teams are the Universities of Alaska at Anchorage and at Fairbanks. They belong to the National Collegiate Athletic Association (NCAA), Division II. Among their men's and women's sports are basketball and alpine skiing. There are also professional hockey teams and senior sports divisions. Dog sledding is a favorite Alaskan sport, and races are held throughout the state each year.

Sarah Hansen was named the Rocky Mountain Intercollegiate Ski Association Women's Nordic Skier of the week in January 2004.

PROFESSIONAL SPORTS

The Fairbanks Ice Dogs are an Alaskan professional hockey team and plays at home in the Big Dipper Arena. It belongs to the American Western Hockey League. The Anchorage Aces, another professional hockey team, play in the Sullivan Arena in Anchorage. It is a member of the West Coast Hockey League.

COLLEGE SPORTS

The University of Alaska at Anchorage teams are called the Seawolves. In 2004, the women's basketball team was the Great Northwest Athletic Conference champions. In 1990 and 2003, the team won the Great Alaska Shootout. Leslie Boyd, a women's cross-country ski team and cross-country

Nanook's men's basketabll is played in the Patty Center, located on th UAF campus.

running team member, was the 2003 NCAA Woman of the Year. In January 2004, Sarah Hansen became the first American woman to win the ten-kilometer freestyle ski race in a Rocky Mountain Intercollegiate Ski Association race since 2001.

The University of Alaska at Fairbanks teams are called the Nanooks. In 2004, the men's basketball team won its division, and in 2003, it won the Great Northwest Athletic Conference championship.

Iditarod Trail Sled Dog Race

The Iditarod is a 1,160-mile dogsled race from Anchorage to Nome. The first race was run in 1972 in memory of the January 1925 run made by a dog named Balto. Balto was the lead dog for six mushers that brought medicine to Nome in –40°F temperatures to stop deaths from diphtheria. Men and women who drive dogsleds are known as mushers. Gary Paulson, a well-known children's book author, raced twice in the Iditarod. Paulson wrote several books, including *Woodsong, Winterdance: The Fine Madness of Running the Iditarod,* and *Puppies, Dogs, and Blue Northers,* about dogs and dogsleds. Alaskan Susan Butcher, born on December 26, 1956, became a famous dogsled racer. She won the Iditarod in 1986, 1987, 1988, and again in 1990. She is the only woman to win the race three years in a row.

Alaska's Businesses and Products

Many businesses in Alaska center on the state's natural resources. Gold, silver, and copper mining is big business in the state. The oil business began after the discovery of petroleum in 1896. Other businesses include the fishing and lumber industries, the government, and the tourist industry.

MINING AND QUARRYING

Alaska mines the largest amount of zinc in the United States. Alaska produces about 50 percent of all the zinc in the United States. The largest silver mine, Green Creek Mine in southeastern Alaska, provides more than seventeen percent of the total silver in the country. The state also has the nation's largest raw gold production, with more than 262,000 ounces. More than 1.5 million tons of coal is produced each year. Half of this coal fuels Alaska's power plants in the Central Region. The rest of the coal is exported outside the state.

ALASKA'S PETROLEUM

The petroleum industry contributes about 85 percent of the state's income. At least 25 percent of U.S.-produced petroleum products are from Alaska. This business is important because it provides people with many types of jobs. Because of this vast supply of petroleum, the United States has to depend less on other countries for petroleum.

ALASKAN PIPELINE

The Trans-Alaska Pipeline is a major means of transporting petroleum across the largest U.S. state. The pipeline, completed in 1977, stretches 800 miles across the state over three mountain ranges and more than 800 rivers and streams. The pipeline begins in Prudhoe Bay, the biggest oil field in North America. It is located along the Arctic coast of northern Alaska. The pipeline transports approximately 88,000 barrels of oil each hour as it winds its way south to Valdez. It is then loaded onto ships to go to other parts of the United States.

Alaska produces more petroleum than any other state in the United States.

FISHING

Alaska ranks first in the United States in commercial fishing. Alaska catches more than four times the amount

Alaskan Permanent Fund

In 1971, the Alaska Native Claims Settlement Act gave ownership of 44 million acres of land and $963 million to Native Alaskans. The money was divided and invested to give the Native Alaskans money earned from their own lands, because they had given up claims to their original oil-rich lands. The Permanent Fund, an account with 25 percent of all mineral lease profits, provides these funds. One-third of this fund goes to citizens who are eighteen years of age or older. Each citizen may apply every year for the $1,100 payment.

The applicant must be a resident of Alaska only and not of another state. He or she cannot receive benefits from another state.

Alaska's ports are filled with fishing vessels of all sizes.

of fish that Louisiana, the second-ranked state, does. Most of the state's catch is shipped to other states. The sea animals most used for food are salmon, crab, shrimp, cod, trout, halibut, herring, and clams. Alaska provides most of the salmon, crab, halibut, and herring consumed in the United States.

TIMBER INDUSTRY

Construction of the first paper mill began in Ketchikan in 1954. The timber industry is centered along the coastal forest in the southeast and the boreal, or subarctic, forest in the Central Uplands and Lowlands. Hundreds of people work in the timber industry, and the government earns millions of dollars each year. The federal government receives 51 percent of the profits from timber harvested on federal-owned lands; the state, the university, and local governments get 25 percent; native corporations get 24 percent; and other private landowners get 0.4 percent.

AGRICULTURE

Alaska supplies almost 85 percent of the fresh fruits and vegetables and almost 100 percent of the food products that are needed in the state. There are dairies for milk products, poultry ranches for fowl products, and 750 acres of potato farms. Alaska's potatoes are sweeter because they have a shorter growing time. A Montana family, the Keasters, established the first Alaskan cattle ranch in 1954. In 2002, the ranch had 11,500 cattle, 1,200 hogs, 1,100 sheep with 4,000 pounds of wool, and 15,000 reindeer.

Attractions and Landmarks

Alaska offers both natural and human-made attractions for its citizens and visitors.

NATIONAL PARKS

Alaska has thirteen national parks, more than any other state. One of the most visited parks is Glacier Bay National Park and Preserve, situated on nearly 3.2 million acres in the southeastern part of the state. Each year, over 300,000 people visit the area to see ocean and land animals in their natural habitat. At nearby Tongass National Forest, visitors can see the enormous Mendenhall Glacier, one of the largest piedmont glaciers in the world. Icebergs, both large and small, break off from the glacier's leading edge, or face. Helicopters take visitors through the valleys formed by rivers of ice and then land on the glacier. People are able to tour the glacier by walking on its surface with special boots that prevent slipping.

Denali National Park and Preserve is north of Anchorage. Trains take passengers along the base of Mount McKinley on a round-trip ride through these mountains. People view the scenery and animals through the many windows of special train cars, called viewing cars. They enjoy the native wildlife, such as moose, caribou, and bald eagles. Hiking, mountain climbing, skiing, and riding snowmobiles are popular attractions for the park's visitors.

The Church of the Holy Ascension is listed on the National Register of Historic Places.

HOLY ASCENSION OF OUR LORD CATHEDRAL

One of the state's oldest churches is found on Unalaska Island in the southwestern part of the state. The present structure was built in 1896, but the original church on this site was built in 1808. Services are sung and chanted in the Aleut language and in English. Everyone stands during the services, women on the left side and the men on the right.

THE INSIDE PASSAGE

The Inside Passage, the chain of islands in southeastern Alaska, stretches for about 1,000 miles. It is a favorite place for tourists to see Alaska's unique traits. Cruise ships travel this passage and move north to Anchorage then south to Vancouver, Canada. Visitors enjoy Ketchikan with its many **totems,** Juneau with its nearby glaciers, and Skagway, which shows what the gateway to the gold rush territories was like in the late 1890s. Other attractions are the snow-covered mountains and places such as Glacier Bay, where visitors can see icebergs, sea otters, whales, porpoises, and bald eagles.

Whale watching is a favorite pastime for tourists who cruise through the Inside Passage.

In the southeast, Skagway attracts those interested in the late 1890s gold rush days. This old mining town has kept the fronts of their buildings as if they were still in the late 1880s. The White Pass and Yukon Route Scenic Railway takes people through the valleys and into the mountains that begin the Yukon Territory. It is a narrow gauge railroad with a fourteen-inch set of tracks. The original engine and cars are

Places to See in Alaska

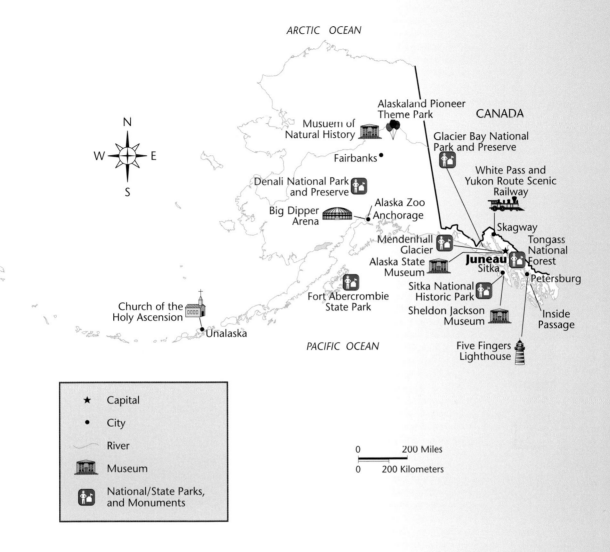

ARCTIC OCEAN

CANADA

Alaskaland Pioneer Theme Park

Musuem of Natural History

Fairbanks

Glacier Bay National Park and Preserve

White Pass and Yukon Route Scenic Railway

Denali National Park and Preserve

Big Dipper Arena

Alaska Zoo Anchorage

Skagway

Tongass National Forest

Mendenhall Glacier

Juneau
Sitka

Alaska State Museum

Petersburg

Church of the Holy Ascension

Fort Abercrombie State Park

Sitka National Historic Park

Sheldon Jackson Museum

Inside Passage

Unalaska

PACIFIC OCEAN

Five Fingers Lighthouse

★ Capital

• City

River

Museum

National/State Parks, and Monuments

0   200 Miles

0   200 Kilometers

sometimes used. Museums, shops, and saloons with residents working the jobs offer a view of a past time.

Alaska's lighthouses are a favorite tourist stop. In 1902, the first federal lighthouse, Five Fingers Lighthouse, was built in Frederick Sound near Petersburg. Lighthouses are located in foggy and dangerous areas to protect the ships and sailors traveling around the many islands and through the shallow waters.

NORTHERN LIGHTS

The aurora borealis, or **northern lights**, resembles a neon light show in the night sky. The interaction of par-

The northern lights are unique to the world's polar regions.

ticles in the atmosphere above the earth's magnetic poles causes this display of lights more than 60 miles above the earth's surfaces. Alaska's residents and visitors to the state can view the northern lights between September and April each year.

THE UNIVERSITY OF ALASKA MUSEUM

The University of Alaska Museum in Fairbanks is the only natural history museum in Alaska. In 1926, Otto William Geist began the museum when he started collecting Native Alaskan artifacts. Among its unique attractions are the remains of a 36,000-year-old bison mummy, woolly mammoths, bears, and wolves. The museum grounds display totem poles, sculptures, and a Russian blockhouse.

"Lizzie" the Dinosaur Fossil

On display in the University of Alaska Museum in Fairbanks is the oldest known dinosaur skeleton found in Alaska. The skeleton is that of a duckbill dinosaurs, also known as a hadrosaur. It was named "Lizzie" after the daughter of the woman who discovered the bones in 1994 in the Talkeetna Mountains.

Map of Alaska

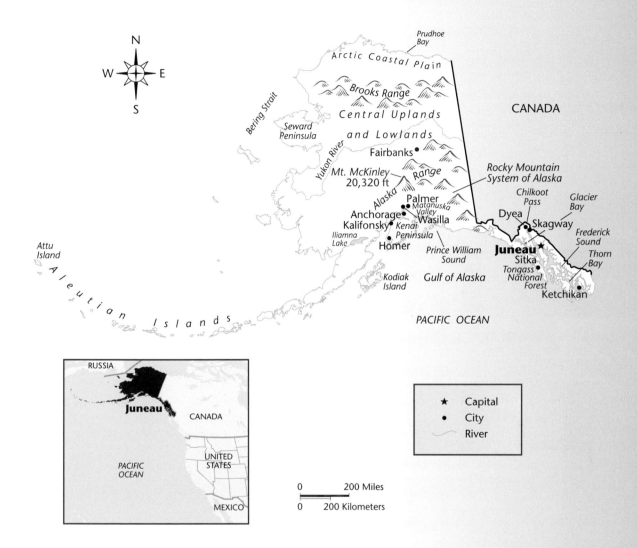

ARCTIC OCEAN

N
W · E
S

Prudhoe Bay

Arctic Coastal Plain

Brooks Range

Central Uplands

and Lowlands

Bering Strait

Seward Peninsula

Yukon River

Fairbanks

Mt. McKinley 20,320 ft

Range

Alaska

Palmer
Matanuska Valley
Anchorage
Kalifonsky
Wasilla
Kenai Peninsula
Iliamna Lake
Homer

Prince William Sound

CANADA

Rocky Mountain System of Alaska

Chilkoot Pass
Glacier Bay
Dyea
Skagway
Frederick Sound
Thorn Bay

Juneau
Sitka
Tongass National Forest

Ketchikan

Gulf of Alaska

Attu Island

Aleutian Islands

Kodiak Island

PACIFIC OCEAN

RUSSIA

Juneau

CANADA

PACIFIC OCEAN

UNITED STATES

MEXICO

★	Capital
•	City
⌇	River

0   200 Miles
0   200 Kilometers

Glossary

Arctic Circle the parallel of latitude that is 66 1/2° north of the equator and that circles the northern frigid zone

bush pilot a person who flies a small airplane to and from remote areas

Civil War the war between the northern states, called the Union, and the southern states, known as the Confederacy, fought between 1861 and 1865

climate the average weather of a place, as exhibited by temperature, wind speed, and precipitation

Confederate of or relating to the Confederate States of America; a soldier who fought for the South during the Civil War in the United States (1861–1865)

contiguous the condition of being connected

federal government the government of the United States

felony a serious crime, which is usually punishable by a penalty of more than one year in jail in addition to fines

fossil the remains of a plant or animal, preserved from a past geologic age

frontier the region where the settled or developed territory meets unsettled areas

glacier thick, slow-moving sheets of ice

magnetic phenomenon of, relating to, or characterized by the earth's attraction for iron; exhibited by both magnets and electric currents; and characterized by fields of force

majority a number more than one half of the total

meteor any of the small particles of matter in the solar system that are seen when they burn upon entry into the Earth's atmosphere

nonpartisan ballot an election ballot on which the candidates do not belong to political parties

northern lights lights that occur in the earth's northern hemisphere as a result of particles from the sun bumping into the earth's magnetic field (also known as aurora borealis)

observatory a building or place equipped for observation of natural phenomena (as in astronomy)

peninsula a portion of land surrounded by water on three sides

permafrost a frozen layer of soil below the surface in the frigid regions of the earth

precipitation hail, rain, sleet, or snow

Richter scale a scale that identifies the intensity of earthquakes, graded from 1 (very weak) to 12 (total destruction)

resident an individual who lives in a place for some length of time

scrimshaw a carved or engraved article, usually made of whale ivory

snowshoe a light oval frame (usually wood or aluminum) that is made with crossed thongs or synthetic material and attached to the foot to enable a person to walk on soft snow without sinking

strait a narrow passage of water that connects two larger bodies of water

temperate moderate; not extreme or excessive; mild

totem an object (such as an animal or plant) that serves as the emblem of a family or clan and is often a reminder of its ancestry; a usually carved or painted representation of such an object

tundra a level treeless plain found in arctic and sub-arctic regions, which consists of black mucky soil and a permanently frozen subsoil, with vegetation of mosses, lichens, herbs, and dwarf shrubs

veto to reject a bill so that it does not become a law

whiteout a weather condition in a snow-covered area (as a polar region) in which no object casts a shadow, the horizon cannot be seen, and only dark objects are visible

World War II (1939–1945) the war between the Allies (Great Britain, France, Russia, and the United States) and the Axis (Germany, Italy, and Japan)

More Books to Read

Dubois, Muriel L. *Alaska Facts and Symbols.* Mankato, Minn.: Capstone Press, 2003.

Edmonds, Margot, and Ella E. Clark. *Voices of the Winds: Native American Legends.* New York: Facts On File, 1989.

Murphy, Claire Rudolf. *A Child's Alaska.* Anchorage: Alaska Northwest Books, 1994.

Norman, Howard, ed. *Northern Tales: Traditional Stories of Eskimo and Indian Peoples.* New York: Pantheon Books, 1990.

Index

About the Authors

Judy A. Henry is a middle school communications teacher in south-central Kansas. Not only is she a world traveler but she also teaches exchange students and has visiting students and teacher interns from around the world in her home and her classroom.

D. J. Ross is a writer and educator with more than 30 years of experience in education. He has lived in many states and frequently has visited other areas of the country, including Alaska. He lives in the Midwest with his three basset hounds.